Book Projects to Send Home

Grade 2

Published by Instructional Fair
an imprint of Carson-Dellosa Publishing

Authors: Lori Sanders & Linda Kimble
Editor: Cary Malaski

Instructional Fair
An imprint of Carson-Dellosa Publishing LLC
P.O. Box 35665
Greensboro, NC 27425 USA

Printed in Minster, Ohio USA • All rights reserved. ISBN 978-0-7424-2732-7 04-144177784

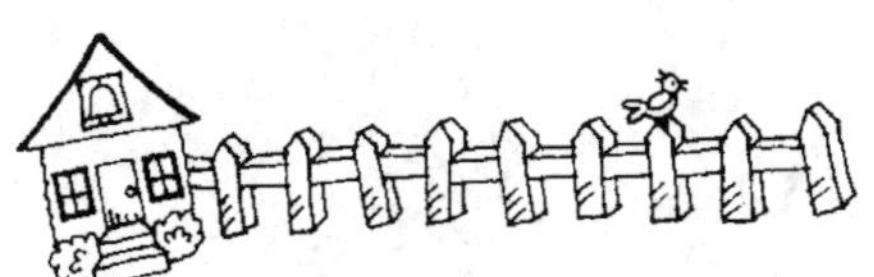

Table of Contents

Book Project Activities

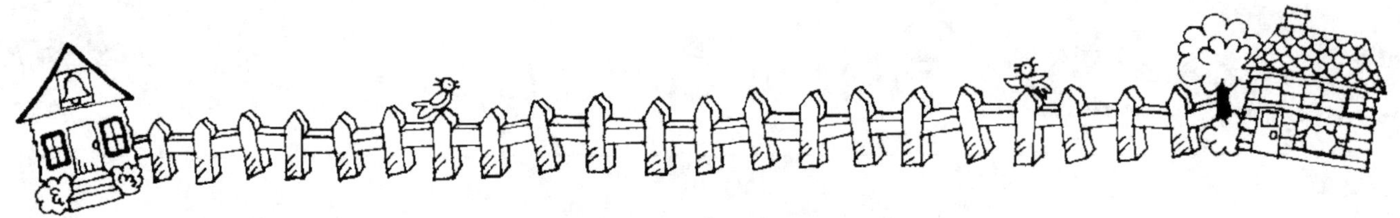

Introduction

School-to-home book projects are a wonderful means of encouraging early readers. In *Book Projects to Send Home,* you will find ten creative book project ideas for students to construct at home with the help of parents. Once completed, each project is returned to school to be shared with the class. Designed to develop early reading skills, the projects allow students to touch upon their various learning styles through art, composition, and oral expression.

Here is a blueprint for using this book's resources:

1. There are two letters to inform parents of your program plans. Launch your Book Projects program with the *Letter to Send Home* on page 5. It is important to enlist parental involvement at the beginning of the school year, and a welcome letter is a great way to do this. Send the *Book Projects Supply List* note on page 6 at the same time. This gives parents advance notice of the art supplies they'll need to have on hand for the projects in this book.
2. Each book project includes a sheet of instructions that explains the project in detail, lists needed materials, provides step-by-step instructions for completing the project, and details the manner in which work will be shared in class. This page also helps parents and students organize their work before assembling it. In addition, there is a pattern page to accompany each project.
3. The *How did I do?* page provides a simple graphic means for self-assessment. Parents may assist with this assessment. This page includes a note for parents to fill out and return, stating that they have received the project instructions so there are no misunderstandings later on in the project. Because you will want to receive this note promptly, be sure to send the *How did I do?* sheet home along with each set of project instructions.
4. To ensure success with the projects at home, teachers are encouraged to model all processes before students take the assignment home. Modeling helps build student confidence and encourages 100 percent participation.

Incorporating this fun and easy school-to-home connection will be a worthwhile complement to your classroom reading instruction. Each completed project lends itself to sharing with the class, either orally or visually. You will be thrilled with the way your students demonstrate creativity and understanding through their work.

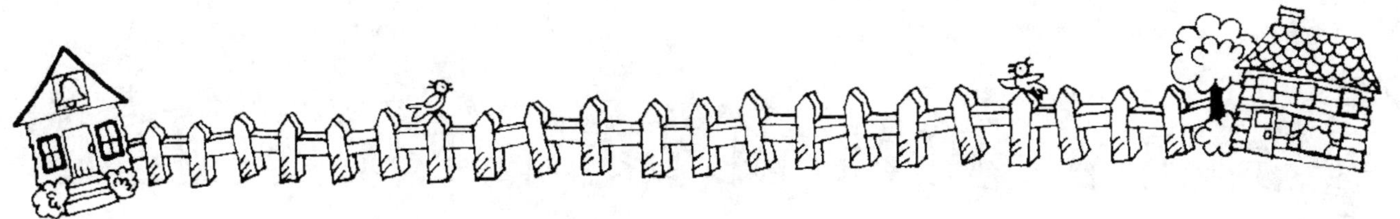

Dear Parents,

Throughout the year, you will be asked to select and read a book with your child. Then you will complete a creative book project together. These book projects involve art, composition, and oral expression. They are designed to demonstrate your child's reading and/or listening comprehension.

Each time you are asked to complete a project with your child, you will receive a list of the necessary materials, instructions for completing the project, the due date, and an explanation of the method we will use to share the projects in class. A self-evaluation sheet will also be included. Discuss each question on this sheet with your child and circle the appropriate smiley face together. Send this sheet back to class with the project.

Please sign and return the form at the bottom of the self-evaluation page. This shows me that each student has received and understands the project requirements.

I also suggest that you assemble a tool kit of materials to be used throughout the year for our projects. A complete list, including extras, is provided on the accompanying sheet.

I look forward to seeing your child's reading skills grow and am confident that these projects will help foster that growth.

Sincerely,

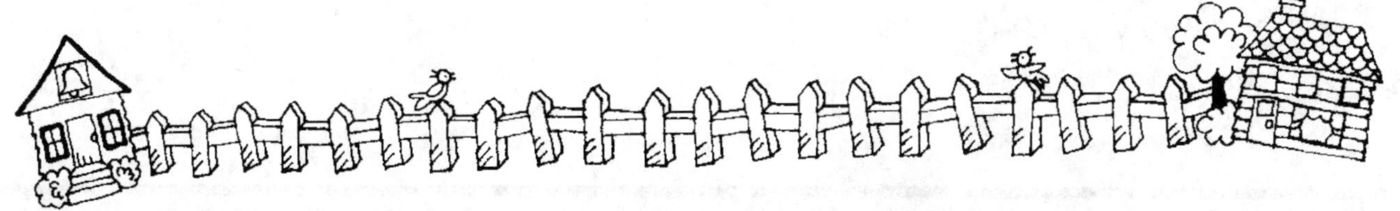

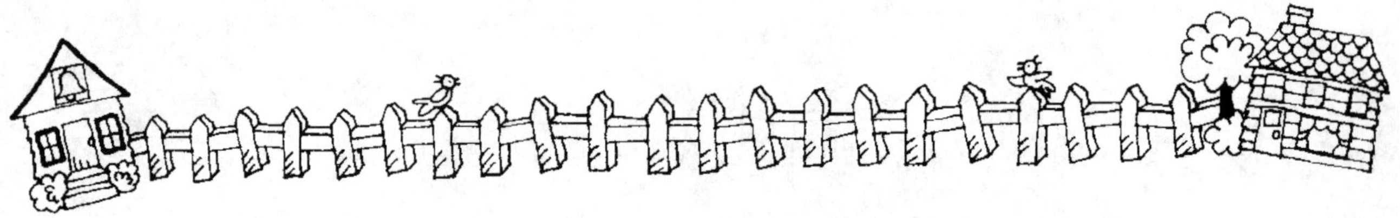

Book Projects Supply List

Dear Parents,
As we begin our school year and prepare to launch our *Book Projects to Send Home* program, I would like to take this opportunity to give you a list of the supplies you and your child will be needing to complete the projects. Knowing what you will need will help you and your child get started on the project as soon as it is assigned.

You will see that this list includes the basic supplies needed, as well as some extras. The extra supplies are not necessary, but your child can use these to enhance his or her creation to make it even more unique!

Basics

- crayons, pencils, and markers
- one shoebox
- one empty cardboard food canister
- one $8\frac{1}{2}$" x 12" or larger envelope
- two $8\frac{1}{2}$" x 11" sheets of paper
- glue
- scissors
- clear tape, duct tape, and masking tape
- stapler
- ruler
- construction paper (white and colored)
- poster board
- one cardboard tube
- roll paper
- one wire hanger
- paper plate (9" diameter)
- recycled wrapping paper
- clean plastic bags

Extras

- stickers
- small beads and buttons
- trim scraps, such as lace, ribbon, or rickrack
- metallic art pens
- corrugated cardboard
- paper with different textures, such as rice paper
- aluminum foil
- wax paper
- a bright recycled stamp or a stamp from an exotic location

Character Tube Puppet

Teacher Guide

Skills Covered

- character analysis
- identification of problem and solution
- reading comprehension
- dramatization

Project Description

The focus of this project is characterization. Students construct a character puppet using a cardboard tube for the body. Then they will complete a personality profile sheet focusing on their character's importance to the story and the problem he or she encountered. Each student chooses a favorite statement from the book made by the character. Each student reads or recites in a dramatic voice while displaying the puppet.

Materials to Provide

Collect cardboard tubes for students who don't have access to them at home. Each student will need a copy of the pattern page.

Tips to Introduce

As an introduction to this project, discuss the fact that characters in a story have both physical and personality traits. Discuss the different ways we get to know a character—through physical description, comments made by other characters, direct statements by the character, and so on.

Choose the main character from a read-aloud selection and record character traits on a two-column chart labeled *Physical Traits* and *Personality Traits*. Then discuss how students can use this type of information when creating their own puppets. Create an overhead transparency of the pattern sheet and complete it as a class using the same main character.

Classroom Connections

As a get-to-know-your-classmates activity, each student draw a self-portrait at the top of a sheet of paper. Ask them to list their physical and personality traits in two columns. Then have them fold the top of the page over so their portrait doesn't show. Students can take turns reading the profile charts and trying to guess who is being described.

Display and Presentation

Students can introduce their puppets by reciting a favorite line from the book in the character's voices. Attach the puppets to a bulletin board using a thumb tack mounted inside the paper tube. Mount the Personality Profile page next to each student's puppet.

Character Tube Puppet

Dear ______________________________ and family,

Choose a picture book or a chapter book to read together. After reading the book, you will use the main character to create a tube puppet. The character may be a person, an animal, or even an object (such as a robot). Record the traits of the character on the pattern page.

Getting started:

Think about the size you want to make your puppet. Then find a cardboard tube in this size (toilet paper tube, paper towel tube, wrapping paper tube, and so on). You need colored paper, glue or tape, markers or crayons, miscellaneous trim such as yarn or movable eyes, and the pattern page.

Making your project:

1. After reading your book, return the signed form at the bottom of the *How did I do?* page.
2. Find a cardboard tube and cover it with paper. Choose a color that is good for the background.

3. Cut pieces of paper to glue to the tube to make the character's head, arms, feet, and other features such as hair, eyes, and clothing. Leave about a third of the tube at the bottom for the handle.
4. Add details with markers. Attach decorative items, such as yarn or movable eyes, with glue or tape.
5. Fill in the pattern page sheet. Cut around the borders and mount the statements on a piece of cardboard or colored paper.

6. Bring your completed project and the book you read to school.

Sharing your character tube puppet:

You will present your puppet to the class by telling us the title of the book and the main character's name. You will also recite favorite lines that your character said in the book, using the character's voice. We will display the finished puppets and pattern pages.

Character Tube Puppet

Pattern Page

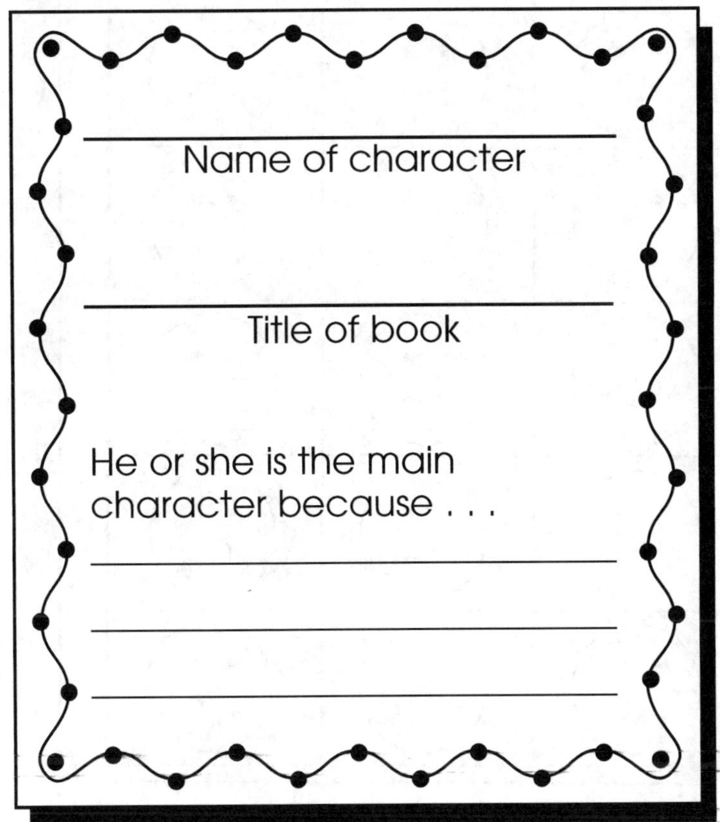

Name of character

Title of book

He or she is the main character because . . .

What problem does the character have?

How is the problem solved?

My favorite thing that this character says is . . .

Character Tube Puppet

How did I do?

My character puppet resembles the main character from the story.	☺	😐	☹
I used information from the story to fill in the pattern page.	☺	😐	☹
I am ready to present my favorite line in the character's voice.	☺	😐	☹
My puppet is neat and colorful.	☺	😐	☹
I gave the project my best effort.	☺	😐	☹

Did you read the book to your child or did your child read the book to you?

____

Other comments:

____

____

____

Comments from Teacher:

____

____

____

____

____

____

Please sign and return

The ______________________ family has received the information for the *Character Tube Puppet* project. We are aware that the project is due on

______________________.

____
Parent Signature

Cylinder Sequence Lit Kit

Teacher Guide

Skills Covered

- sequencing of events
- reading comprehension
- summarizing
- retelling of a story

Project Description

Students use a wide-mouthed container, such as a coffee can, on which to display three main events from a book they have read. They will fill their can with 3–5 objects that will help them retell the story to the class.

Materials to Provide

Collect a variety of round containers so you have extras for students who may not have access to them at home.

Tips to Introduce

Students often struggle in determining the difference between significant and insignificant events in a book. Model this process with a read-aloud book to help students feel more confident with this concept. Students may also have difficulty identifying important objects from the story that will help them in retelling it. Use a familiar fairy tale or folktale to model retelling. You will find that students are often able to give the main events and identify what objects are important to the plot in this genre.

Classroom Connections

Summarizing can be a real challenge for students who want to tell every detail of a story. Over several weeks, introduce the skill of summarizing, emphasizing the fact that not every detail of a book is important.

You can use a variety of materials to teach this skill, such as storybooks, videos, and events that your class has participated in, such as field trips. On chart paper, list all events that children recall. Then discuss why some should be kept and some should be eliminated.

Also model using an object from the story to help reenact or retell the story. For example, explain why displaying a tiny bowl during your presentation of *Goldilocks and the Three Bears* would be helpful in describing the story.

Display and Presentation

Create an area in your classroom to display the lit kits. Students will enjoy showing off their lit kits to other students and adults who visit the classroom.

Cylinder Sequence Lit Kit

Dear ______________________________ and family,

Find a picture book or chapter book to read together. You will use this book to make a lit kit in a canister. The outside of the canister will be decorated with pictures showing the main events of the story. The inside of the canister will contain objects to help you retell the story to our class.

Getting started:

You need a wide-mouthed round container such as a coffee can, a piece of light-colored paper to fit around the outside of the container, glue or tape, string or thread, and markers or crayons. If you decide to make props to place inside, you will need some recycled materials from around the house. Use the pattern page to make tags to attach to each one of your props.

Making your project:

1. After reading your fiction book, return the signed form at the bottom of the *How did I do?* page.
2. Measure the height and diameter of your container. Cut a piece of paper to fit your container.
3. Divide the paper into four sections. On the first section, write the title and author of the book. Decorate this section with a picture from the book.

4. The other three sections will show pictures of three main events from the book—one event from the beginning, one from the middle, and one from the end. Choose scenes that are interesting and important to the story. Use a lot of detail and fill the space completely. Label the sections *Beginning, Middle,* and *End*. Glue this page around the container.
5. Think of 3–5 small items you could make or find to put in the container to help you retell the story. Fill in the pattern page so each prop has a tag. Attach the tags to the props with string, thread, or tape.
6. Bring your completed project to school.

Sharing your cylinder sequence lit kit:

Practice telling your story to an adult so you will be ready to retell it to our class. In your presentation, use all of the objects inside the canister and the pictures on the outside.

Cylinder Sequence Lit Kit

Pattern Page

Cylinder Sequence Kit

Made by

Title of book

Date

Prop Profile

Object Name:

I chose this object to help retell the story because . . .

Prop Profile

Object Name:

I chose this object to help retell the story because . . .

Prop Profile

Object Name:

I chose this object to help retell the story because . . .

Prop Profile

Object Name:

I chose this object to help retell the story because . . .

Prop Profile

Object Name:

I chose this object to help retell the story because . . .

Cylinder Sequence Lit Kit

How did I do?

I illustrated important scenes from the beginning, middle, and end of the book I read.			
I can retell the story using the pictures on my can and the objects inside of it.			
My lit kit is neat and colorful.			
I gave the project my best effort.			
I brought my project to school on time.			

Did you read the book to your child or did your child read the book to you?

____

Other comments:

____

____

____

Comments from Teacher:

____

____

____

____

____

____

Please sign and return

The ______________________ family has received the information for the *Cylinder Sequence Lit Kit* project. We are aware that the project is due on ______________________.

____
Parent Signature

Detailed Diorama

Teacher Guide

Skills Covered

- identification of story elements
- reading comprehension

Project Description

Students focus on the story elements of characters, setting, and plot as they design a three-dimensional diorama. Using a box and items from home, they incorporate details from a key event of their choice into their diorama. The pattern page provides opportunities to write about discovered story elements.

Materials to Provide

Provide a copy of the pattern page for each student. All other materials needed will come from home.

Tips to Introduce

This project emphasizes the literary terminology of *event, setting,* and *plot.* You should assist students as they refine their understanding of the role that plot plays in creating a story line. Students need opportunities to chart, compare, and contrast story events to develop a sense of sequence and to understand the importance of the setting to a story.

You can emphasize the impact that setting plays in a book by taking a familiar story and asking students to write about how the story would change if the setting were different. For example, "What if Goldilocks met the three bears in a city, not in the woods?"

To demonstrate how important the sequence of events is to the story line, make sequence cards for several events in a familiar story. Then rearrange or change the events and ask what impact this has on the story. By doing this, you are helping students develop an appreciation of the effort and planning an author invests when writing a story.

Classroom Connections

If this is the first time students have created a diorama, include the making of a diorama in one of your units. Small groups of students can build dioramas related to a unit, such as habitats of animals or landforms.

Display and Presentation

These projects provide a perfect opportunity for your class to build a classroom Book Brag Museum. Students can tell visiting guests about their books and why they included the details they chose for their dioramas. They can be book experts as they introduce others to these stories.

Detailed Diorama

Dear ________________________________ and family,

The location an author chooses for the setting of a story is an important part of any book. For this at-home book project, you will read a fiction book with an interesting setting that you can re-create in a diorama. You will create a three-dimensional diorama that shows an important event in your story, while paying close attention to the details of the setting. You will also map out the key events of your story on your pattern page. Your diorama will be displayed in our classroom Book Brag Museum.

Getting started:

You need a shoebox and the pattern page. Look around your house for materials you can use to reconstruct a detailed three-dimensional scene from your story.

Making your project:

1. As you read the book, record the sequence of events on scratch paper. Have an adult help you revise and edit your list. Return the signed form at the bottom of the *How did I do?* page.
2. Fill in the pattern page. Cut out each box.
3. Collect the materials you need to illustrate the setting and characters as they appeared in a key event from your story. Remember to add special details to make your diorama three-dimensional, such as clay models of characters, foil for a pond or lake, cotton balls for clouds or snow, and so on. Use all of the space within the box.
4. Decorate the outside walls of the diorama. Glue the two small pattern page pieces onto the two ends of your box. Attach the large pattern box to the back of your diorama.
5. Bring your completed project to school.

Sharing your diorama:

We will put all of our dioramas on display in our Book Brag Museum and invite others to visit and learn about the books we chose.

Detailed Diorama

Pattern Page

The Main Events

First, ____

____

____

Then, ____

____

____

Finally, ____

____

____

Cast of Characters

____

____

____

____

____

____

____

____

____

Description of Setting

____

____

____

____

____

____

____

____

____

Detailed Diorama

How did I do?

My diorama is detailed and three-dimensional.	☺	😐	☹
I filled in the pattern page with information from the book.	☺	😐	☹
My diorama is neat and colorful.	☺	😐	☹
I gave the project my best effort.	☺	😐	☹
I brought my project to school on time.	☺	😐	☹

Did you read the book to your child or did your child read the book to you?

____

Other comments:

____

____

____

Comments from Teacher:

____

____

____

____

____

____

Please sign and return

The ______________________ family has received the information for the *Detailed Diorama* project. We are aware that the project is due on ______________________.

____
Parent Signature

Face-to-Face Character Mask

Teacher Guide

Skills Covered

- character analysis
- reading comprehension

Project Description

After reading a fiction book, students select an interesting character to illustrate as a faceless mask. It's faceless because each child will incorporate his or her own face into the mask opening to bring a character to life. Students complete project tags and a descriptive paragraph about each character. They assume the role of the character and answer interview questions as that character.

Materials to Provide

Each student will need a large piece of poster board and a copy of the pattern page. The rest of the materials will come from home.

Tips to Introduce

Working on visual-spatial concepts can be challenging. Discuss the importance of using the entire poster board. You may want to create a faceless mask as a class before assigning it for home.

Students will have a chance to write from a character's point of view. Find ways to practice this skill in advance using read-aloud selections and familiar stories. Ask students to write journal responses as if they were the story character speaking aloud.

Classroom Connections

Provide the opportunity to make puppets or masks in class to support this project. Help get students excited about role-playing. Role-playing can be applied to nearly every content area and can make the learning process fun and purposeful. For example, when you study units in science, look for ways students can role-play as biologists, researchers, geologists, and so on. Students often become more actively engaged in learning and their understanding deepens through role-playing.

Display and Presentation

Bring a camera to class to take pictures of students in their masks. Encourage role-playing as students wear their masks and answer questions in character. Create a bulletin board display of the pictures.

Face-to-Face Character Mask

Dear ______________________________ and family,

Have you ever peeked through the face hole on a statue at an amusement park? Now is your chance to create your own mask. Read a fiction book that has an interesting character. You will draw a large body without a face so your face becomes the character's face.

Getting started:

You need the piece of poster board from class, the pattern page, glue, and markers or crayons. You also should collect materials such as yarn, fabric scraps, buttons, lace, ribbon, and wrapping paper.

Making your project:

1. Return the signed form at the bottom of the *How did I do?* page.
2. The main character of your story will be the model for your mask. Cut an oval opening the size of your face on the top part of the poster board. Then draw the details of the head and upper body to create your mask.
3. Finish your mask by adding materials. Glue on yarn for hair or beads for a necklace. Use wrapping paper or fabric for clothing.

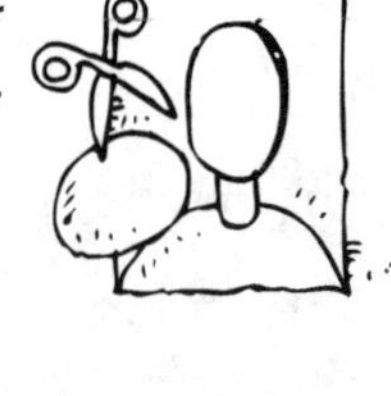

4. Use your pattern page to complete the written portion of the project. Attach the project tag and character description to the front corners of your mask. Glue character questions to the back of your poster board.

5. Using your family as the audience, practice acting like your character. Be prepared to answer the questions on the pattern page as if you were the character from your book.
6. Bring your completed project to school.

Sharing your character mask:

Using your mask, you will introduce yourself as your book character to our class. Then I will ask you to answer the questions about your character that are listed on the pattern page.

Face-to-Face Character Mask

Pattern Page

Project Tag

____

Title

____

Author

____

Project

____

Date

Character Description

____

____

____

____

____

____

____

____

____

Character Questions

What is the most interesting thing you did in this book?

____

____

____

If you could do one thing differently in the story, what would it be and why?

____

____

____

Face-to-Face Character Mask

How did I do?

I used a variety of materials to make my character mask.			
I can answer questions as the character I chose.			
My mask is neat and colorful.			
I gave the project my best effort.			
I brought my project to school on time.			

Did you read the book to your child or did your child read the book to you?

____

Other comments:

____

____

____

Comments from Teacher:

____

____

____

____

____

____

Please sign and return

The ______________________ family has received the information for the *Face-to-Face Character Mask* project. We are aware that the project is due on

______________________.

____
Parent Signature

Main Character Mobile

Teacher Guide

Skills Covered

- characterization
- identification of story elements
- reading comprehension

Project Description

Gaining an understanding and appreciation of story characters and story plot is the focus of this creative project. Each student uses pattern pieces and materials from home to create a character from a folktale or multicultural story. Students also write diamanté poems and identify the physical and personality traits of the main characters in the stories they read.

Materials to Provide

Each student will need a copy of the pattern page. Provide the paper plate and scrap materials for students who do not have access to these at home.

Tips to Introduce

Review and reinforce the idea of character traits (specifically physical and personality traits) in the context of classroom read-alouds to help build student confidence for this project. Select two or three versions of a fairy tale or folktale and examine the similarities and differences in the main character from each version. Then record the comparisons on large sheets of paper to use as a reference in the classroom. Photocopy this chart and attach it to the project letter sent home so parents understand what students are doing.

Classroom Connections

If this is the first time students have written a diamanté poem, send home an example as a reference. Use yourself as the example and create the poem together as a class.

Display and Presentation

These character mobiles look adorable hanging on a clothesline or in the hallway. They also can be displayed in the school media center. Each student should be asked to introduce his or her character and the book from which the character came.

Main Character Mobile

Dear ______________________________________ and family,

You will create a mobile of a favorite character you have met in a folktale or multicultural story. We will display our mobiles around the room for everyone to enjoy.

Getting started:

You will need a wire hanger, masking tape or glue, a 9" paper plate, markers, crayons, yarn, fabric or wrapping paper scraps, a 9" x 12" piece of poster board, a sheet of white drawing paper, and the pattern page.

Making your project:

1. Read a folktale or multicultural story that features an interesting character. Return the signed form at the bottom of the *How did I do?* page.
2. Make a list of the character's physical and personality traits. You will print these traits on the arms of your mobile in step 4.

3. With markers, scrap material, and yarn, add details to the paper plate. Attach the back of the paper plate to the neck of the wire hanger. This is the face.
4. Draw and color two arms (with hands) on the edges of the poster board and cut them out. Use a black marker to write the character's physical traits on one arm and the personality traits on the other.

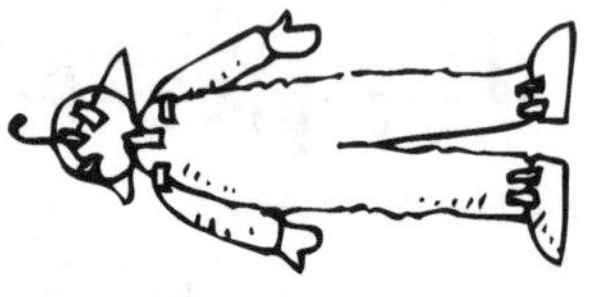

5. Make the body and legs of your character from the rest of the poster board and materials. Attach the body to the hanger and tape on the arms. Attach the completed shoes with tape or glue.

6. Create a poem on the pattern page. Recopy it and attach to your character.
7. Use the *Diamanté Poem* pattern to draft a poem about your character. Recopy your poem to the sheet of white paper. Trim the edges and attach it to your character's body.

Dynamic Diamanté Poem

____

(Name of character)

__________ __________

(2 words that describe the character)

__________ __________ __________

(3 action words about the character)

__________ __________

(2 more describing words)

____

(Name of character)

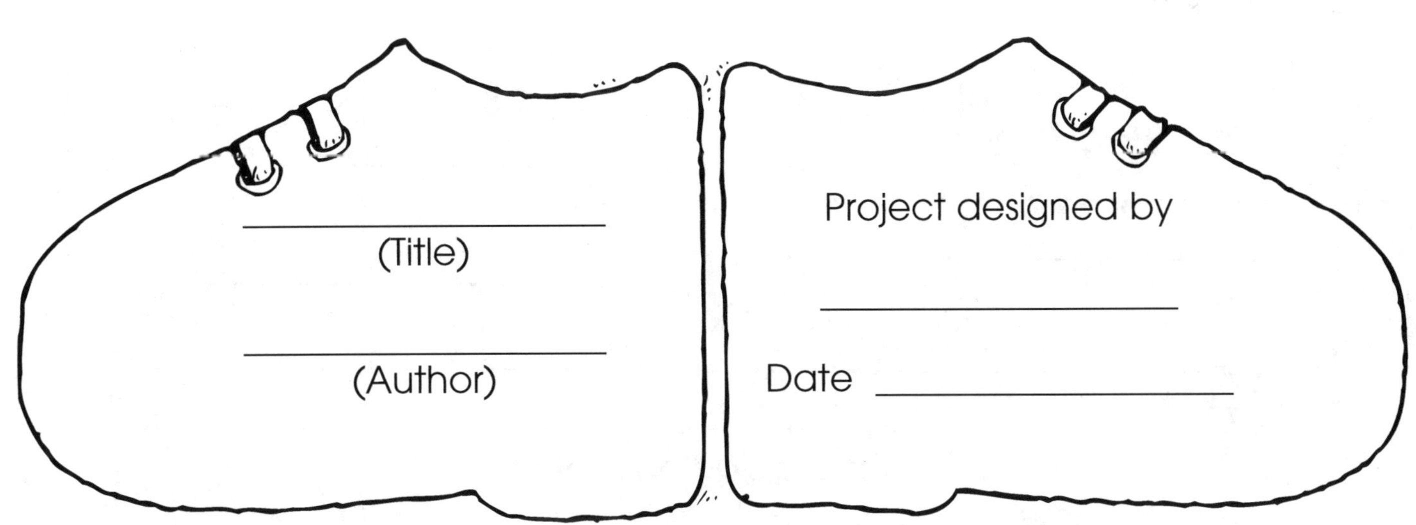

Main Character Mobile

How did I do?

I completed my character pieces and assembled my mobile correctly.			
I wrote a descriptive diamanté poem about the character I chose.			
My mobile is neat and colorful.			
I gave the project my best effort.			
I brought my project to school on time.			

Did you read the book to your child or did your child read the book to you?

____

Other comments:

____

____

____

Comments from Teacher:

____

____

____

____

____

____

Please sign and return

The ______________________ family has received the information for the *Main Character Mobile* project. We are aware that the project is due on

______________________.

____
Parent Signature

Nature's Wonders Accordion Book

Teacher Guide

Skills Covered

- finding information in a nonfiction book
- using adjectives to describe objects
- sentence composition
- reading comprehension

Project Description

Students expand their knowledge and appreciation of nature by creating an accordion book. After choosing an element of nature in which they are interested, they research and answer five questions about their topic. This information, along with a title page and illustrations, make up the seven-page accordion book.

Materials to Provide

Provide a copy of the pattern page for each student. You also may want to provide the poster board pieces, cut to 5" x 6".

Tips to Introduce

Using a science theme in your curriculum, model filling in the pattern page using this theme. Reproduce the pattern page on an overhead transparency and complete it as a class. Or use a K-W-L chart to assess students' prior knowledge about the subject you've selected and to get them thinking about what they want to learn. Then model how to find information on a topic and complete the rest of the chart.

Classroom Connections

Display a number of items from nature, such as rocks, shells, leaves, potatoes, and so on. Let students use their senses to help write definitions for these items. Create lists of adjectives as students handle the objects. Then model sentence composition using words from the lists. Prepare a display of nonfiction books related to nature and encourage students to bring books, posters, articles, and other related items from home. If one topic generates a lot of interest, you can use it to create a classroom accordion book, with each student contributing one page. Let the book zigzag its way down the hallway so passersby can see how excited your students are about research.

Display and Presentation

Students can read their books to each other in pairs or small groups. Or invite special guests, such as parents or grandparents, to your classroom to be the audience. After the presentations, place the books in your classroom library so they are easily accessible.

Nature's Wonders Accordion Book

Dear ______________________________________ and family,

Nature is filled with beautiful sounds and sights. Choose something of interest that is created by nature, such as rocks, flowers, oceans, or forests. Find a nonfiction book on this topic and learn all about it. You will use what you learn to create an accordion book to tell others about this natural wonder.

Getting started:

Gather several sheets of poster board, tape, glue, scissors, and markers or crayons. You also need the pattern page.

Making your project:

1. Choose a subject you want to learn more about. Find a nonfiction book to read together. Return the signed form at the bottom of the *How did I do?* page.
2. As you read the book, write down facts that will help you answer the questions on the pattern page.
3. Cut seven pieces of poster board, 5" x 6" each. Then cut out and glue the questions from the pattern page to the top of each piece of poster board.
4. Write your answers on scratch paper first so you can revise and edit them with an adult. Then write your final answers onto each pattern page square.
5. On the seventh piece of poster board, create an illustration of your topic.
6. Lay the pages side by side from left to right with the title page first, followed by the written pages in numbered order and ending with the illustration. Tape the pages together.
7. Bring your completed project to school.

Sharing your accordion book:

You will share your accordion book with the class by reading it out loud. We will all learn about different elements in nature by listening to each other's books.

Nature's Wonders Accordion Book

Pattern Page

Title Page

Name

Book title

Author

I learned about

1. Name of the element from nature:

Definition:

2. Where can we find this element of nature?

3. Why is it important to people?

4. How can we care for it?

5. What is the most interesting thing you learned about your topic?

How did I do?

I assembled my book in the correct order.	☺	😐	☹
I used complete sentences to answer the questions about my topic.	☺	😐	☹
My book is neat and colorful.	☺	😐	☹
I gave the project my best effort.	☺	😐	☹
I brought my project to school on time.	☺	😐	☹

Did you read the book to your child or did your child read the book to you?

____

Other comments:

____

____

____

Comments from Teacher:

____

____

____

____

____

____

Please sign and return

The ____________________ family has received the information for the *Nature's Wonders Accordion Book* project. We are aware that the project is due on ____________________.

____
Parent Signature

Patchwork of Facts

Teacher Guide

Skills Covered

- finding information in a nonfiction book
- persuasive writing
- patterning

Project Description

Using the pattern page and a 12" x 12" square piece of poster board, each student designs and constructs a patchwork quilt square that features facts from a nonfiction book he or she has selected. The square will include decorative designs using materials from home, three interesting facts, and a sentence convincing others to read the book.

Materials to Provide

Provide a copy of the pattern page and a 12" x 12" piece of poster board for each student in your class.

Tips to Introduce

Provide a quilt or ask students to bring in a quilt from home. If possible, invite someone to your classroom to demonstrate the art of quilting. The goal is to develop an appreciation for the artistry and perseverance it takes to construct a quilt. An awareness of the variety of designs and historical importance of quilts can be emphasized through the sharing of books as well as actual examples. Discuss the importance of planning a layout and giving one's best effort when creating a patchwork square.

Classroom Connections

Quilts are a great way to develop visual-spatial skills involving patterning and geometry. In your art center, you can provide scraps of wallpaper and wrapping paper old greeting cards, and solid-colored paper precut into different geometric shapes. Provide background squares of differing sizes so students are challenged to create a variety of layouts. Attach a sample quilt square to the letter home so parents can see a visual example of the possibilities.

Look in your school or local library to find a wide variety of children's books on the art of quilting.

Display and Presentation

Have students share their quilt squares in small groups. Help each small group assemble their squares to create a group quilt. Then put the quilt blocks from each small group together to create a whole-class quilt that can be hung on the wall or a clothesline.

Patchwork of Facts

Dear ______________________________ and family,

After reading a nonfiction book of your choice, you will design a patchwork quilt square on paper that will teach your classmates three interesting facts about the topic you chose to read about.

Getting started:

Use the pattern page pieces to make four triangles and a diamond for your patchwork square. You may use colored construction paper, wrapping paper, or wallpaper scraps to fill in plain and patterned contrasts between the written pieces. Glue your pieces to a 12" x 12" poster board square.

Making your project:

1. Select a nonfiction topic that interests you and find a book about this subject. Return the signed form at the bottom of the *How did I do?* page.

2. Use scratch paper to write down seven facts that might work well on your quilt square. Ask an adult to help you turn these facts into sentences.

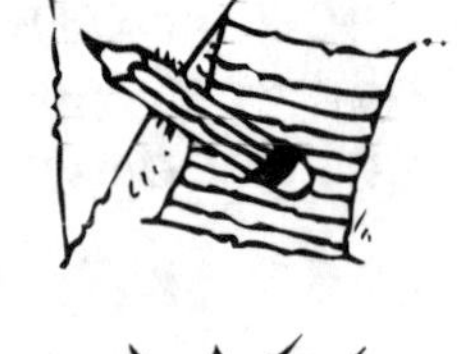

3. Select the three most interesting facts you have learned. Record each fact on a triangle pattern piece.
4. Complete the diamond on the pattern page.
5. Cut apart the pattern page so you have five separate pieces (four triangles and one diamond). Lay the completed pattern page pieces on the poster board. Move them around until you like the design.

6. Glue your plain and patterned pieces between the pattern page pieces to finish the quilt square.
7. Bring your completed project to school.

Sharing your patchwork of facts:

We'll piece our squares together to create a class quilt of facts and a giant reading board. What information we will share!

Patchwork of Facts

Pattern Page

Fact One

Fact Two

You should read about

____

because . . .

____

____

____

____

____

____

Fact Three

Title: ______________

Author: ______________

Project by: ______________

How did I do?

I picked three interesting facts about my nonfiction topic.	☺	😐	☹
I used different plain and patterned pieces to decorate my quilt square.	☺	😐	☹
My quilt square is neat and colorful.	☺	😐	☹
I gave the project my best effort.	☺	😐	☹
I brought my project to school on time.	☺	😐	☹

Did you read the book to your child or did your child read the book to you?

____

Other comments:

____

____

____

Comments from Teacher:

____

____

____

____

____

____

Please sign and return

The _______________ family has received the information for the *Patchwork of Facts* project. We are aware that the project is due on _______________.

____
Parent Signature

Poetry Pal Puzzle

Teacher Guide

Skills Covered

- identifying rhyming words
- editing
- reading comprehension

Project Description

Students read a variety of poetry books before choosing a favorite poem and making a cut-apart puzzle. The pieces of the puzzle will be lines from the chosen rhyming poem. Other students will have the opportunity to put these puzzles together by matching rhyming words and pictures from the student-created borders. Each set of puzzle pieces will be placed in a large envelope, which is decorated on one side with a self-portrait of the Poetry Pal who created the puzzle. The other side will display a copy of the poem, so the puzzle is self-checking. Students also complete a *Poetry Pal Puzzle* pattern page about the poem they chose.

Materials to Provide

Provide the 8 1/2" x 11" envelope and a matching-sized piece of poster board for each student.

Tips to Introduce

Find a rhyming poem that you enjoy and copy it to a large piece of poster board. Make sure each line of the poem takes up only one line of your chart. Then create a related decorative border around the edge. Next, cut the poem into strips and have students resequence them on the floor or in a pocket chart by matching the rhyming words in each line. Fill out the pattern page together.

Classroom Connections

When introducing poetry, share poems that offer a variety of moods. Students particularly enjoy anthologies of humorous poems, which offer a nice break during long days of academic work.

Display a poem of the day or week on a large piece of poster board or on the overhead. After reading the poem once to students, ask them to join in during the second reading. Model using different voices to reflect the mood of the poem and ask students to do the same.

Poets often enjoy sharing their craft. If you or another adult in the building writes poetry, share your rough drafts and final copies with students. Model the fun and endless power of wordplay.

Display and Presentation

Place these puzzles in a box in your reading center. Students can assemble them on the floor or on a tabletop and read them aloud to hear the rhyming sounds.

Poetry Pal Puzzle

Dear ______________________________ and family,

Poems come in so many different shapes and sizes. Read some poems together and enjoy the words you hear and the story that each poem tells. After choosing a favorite poem, you will make a poem puzzle and a Poetry Pal envelope in which to store your puzzle.

Getting started:

You need the pattern page, two pieces of $8\frac{1}{2}$" x 11" paper and a piece of poster board of the same size, a large mailing envelope ($8\frac{1}{2}$" x 11" or larger), scissors, markers or crayons, and glue.

Making your project:

1. Decorate the front of the envelope with a picture of yourself. At the top, write "(your name) is a Poetry Pal." Return the signed form at the bottom of the *How did I do?* page.
2. Choose a short rhyming poem that you really like. On your paper, write the poem two times in your neatest writing. Leave space between each line and leave $\frac{1}{2}$" or more around the edge for a border. Read the finished poems carefully to make sure there are no mistakes.

3. Glue one copy of the poem to the back of your envelope.
4. Draw a border around the second copy of your poem. Color your border and decorate it with pictures of objects from the poem. Glue this copy of the poem to your piece of poster board.
5. Cut the second copy of the poem into strips. Each line of the poem should be one strip and should have a rhyming word at the end of it. Place all of the strips in the envelope. Your classmates can try to put it back together. They can check their work by looking at the whole poem on the back of the envelope. Fill in the pattern page and place it in the envelope with your puzzle.

6. Bring your completed project to school.

Sharing your poetry pal puzzle:

We will put your Poetry Pal Puzzle in a special place in our room so your classmates can try your puzzle and read the poem you chose.

Poetry Pal Puzzle

Pattern Page

The poetry books I read were

(Give title and author for each one)

The poem I picked is called

Include title and author

It is about

I like this poem because

The rhyming words in this poem are

Poetry Pal Puzzle

How did I do?

Each poem strip ends with a rhyming word.			
I filled in the pattern page completely.			
My puzzle is neat and colorful.			
I gave the project my best effort.			
I brought my project to school on time.			

Did you read the book to your child or did your child read the book to you?

____

Other comments:

____

____

____

Comments from Teacher:

____

____

____

____

____

____

Please sign and return

The ________________________ family has received the information for the *Poetry Pal Puzzle* project. We are aware that the project is due on ________________________.

____

Parent Signature

Stuffed Animal Research

Teacher Guide

Skills Covered

- use of a nonfiction book for research
- note taking
- reading comprehension

Project Description

After researching an animal of their choice, students complete the pattern page with information obtained from research. Each student draws and creates a stuffed-paper version of the animal they studied. Then they write a paragraph based on the pattern page information.

Materials to Provide

Provide a copy of the pattern page for each student. If students do not have access to the other items needed, have them on hand to pass out.

Tips to Introduce

Discuss with students that reports and other research-based nonfiction writing must be in the students' original words and must not be information copied from a book. Copy the pattern page to a transparency and model note taking. Show students how to answer the questions in brief phrases or single words. Then guide them in helping you write a complete paragraph using the information from the pattern page.

Classroom Connections

This project lends itself well to the introduction of habitats, or biomes. Survey students to determine which animals have been chosen for the research and then group the animals by habitat. Students can use large sheets of roll paper to draw and paint different habitats, such as a forest, a desert, an ocean, a tundra, grasslands, or wetlands. Display these on the walls in your classroom or in another area in the building that is visible to students in other grades. The stuffed animals can be placed in their habitats when children bring their projects to school.

Display and Presentation

Have students with animals in the same habitat present back-to-back. Invite guests, such as parents and grandparents, to sit in on the presentations.

Display the animals with the corresponding pattern pages so students can learn about different animals and their homes.

Stuffed Animal Research

Dear ___________________________________ and family,

Do you have a favorite animal that lives in the wild or on a farm? This project is your chance to learn more about the animal. Read a nonfiction book about your favorite animal. Collect facts to help you design a stuffed-paper version of your animal. Then you will write a paragraph about the animal you chose.

Getting started:

You need two pieces of large paper, plastic bags or newspaper, paints, chalk or markers, a stapler, and the pattern page.

Making your project:

1. After reading a nonfiction book about an animal, return the signed form at the bottom of the *How did I do?* page. Use the information to draw the animal on a large piece of paper. Add details such as facial features. Then cut out two copies of your animal. The decorated side will be the front of your animal. The other side will be the back.
2. Decide how to color or paint your animal to make it look real. You may want to use a black marker to add some details and shading.
3. Staple the lower edge and two sides of the animal cutouts. Stuff shredded newspaper or plastic bags into the pouch you have created. Use enough stuffing to add dimension, but be careful not to overstuff. Staple the upper edge to finish your animal.
4. Take notes on the pattern page. Then write complete sentences using your information from the pattern page.
5. Combine your sentences into a paragraph.
6. Bring your completed project to school.

Sharing your stuffed animal research:

You will describe your animal while showing us your stuffed animal.

Stuffed Animal Research

Pattern Page

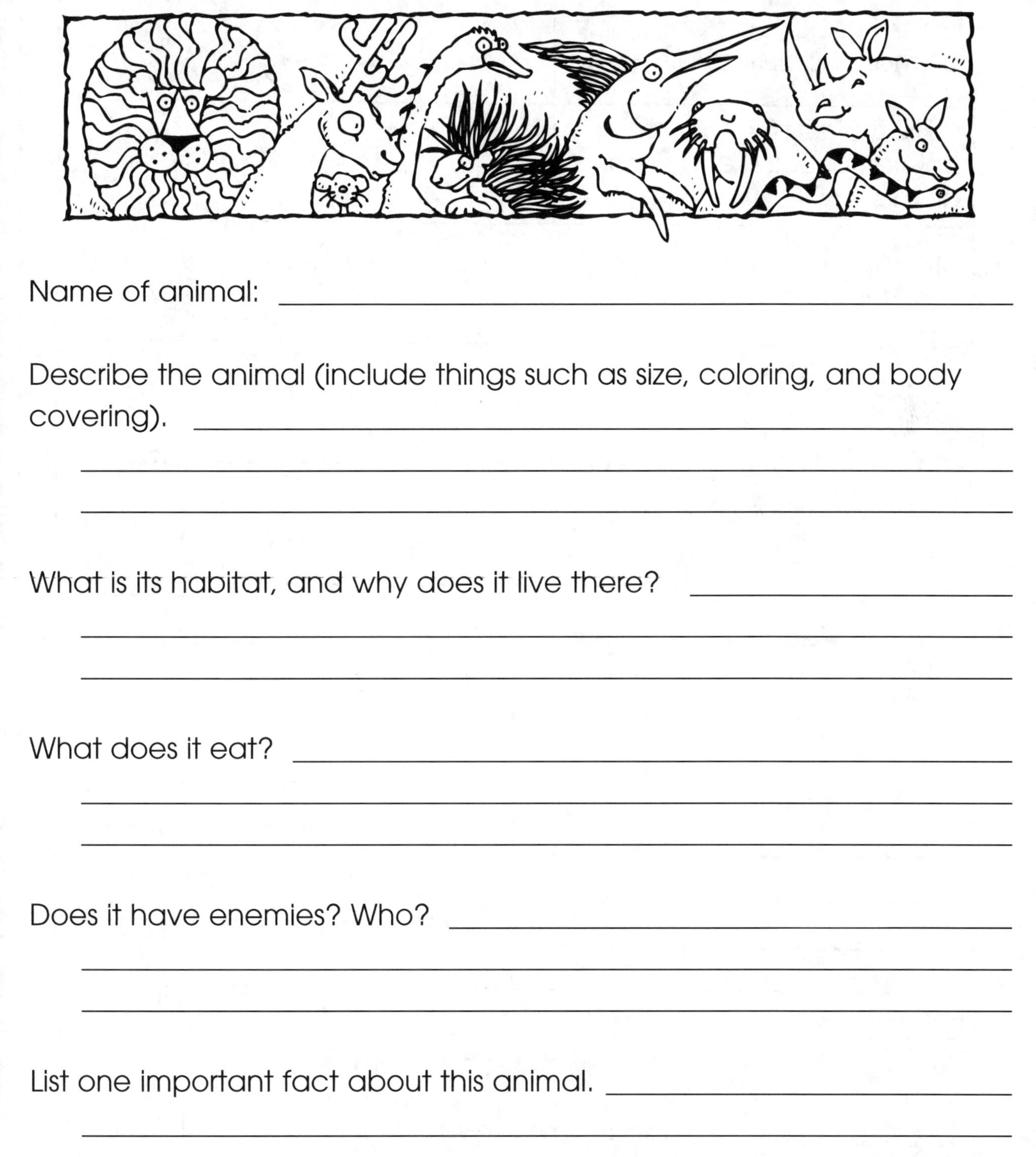

Name of animal: ______________________________

Describe the animal (include things such as size, coloring, and body covering). ______________________________

____

____

What is its habitat, and why does it live there? ______________________________

____

____

What does it eat? ______________________________

____

____

Does it have enemies? Who? ______________________________

____

____

List one important fact about this animal. ______________________________

____

____

Stuffed Animal Research

How did I do?

I researched facts about my animal's habitat and habits.			
I decorated my stuffed animal to look like the real animal.			
My animal is neat and colorful.			
I gave the project my best effort.			
I brought my project to school on time.			

Did you read the book to your child or did your child read the book to you?

____

Other comments:

____

____

____

Comments from Teacher:

____

____

____

____

____

____

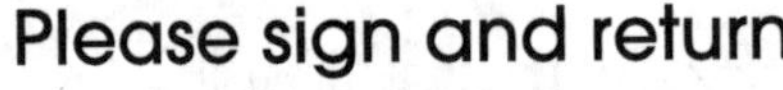

Please sign and return

The __________________________ family has received the information for the *Stuffed Animal Research* project. We are aware that the project is due on

__________________________.

____

Parent Signature

Adventure Thank-You Note

Teacher Guide

Skills Covered

- letter writing
- identifying story elements
- reading comprehension

Project Description

After enjoying an adventure chapter book, students compose a thank-you note to the book characters. Students pretend to have participated in an event from the story and thank the characters for the adventure. Their note will describe the events and setting of the story. Students will also illustrate the event for the front cover of the card.

Materials to Provide

Each student needs a copy of the pattern page and one sheet of 9" x 12" colored construction paper.

Tips to Introduce

Review the terms *setting* and *event* to prepare students for success with this project. Using stories from your reading series or classroom library, identify story elements as a class. Monitor students' understanding of story elements by asking them to record the setting and events of a story they are reading independently or by assigning a story to the class and asking each student to record the setting and events.

Classroom Connections

This project lends itself well to the introduction or review of letter writing. To give the project a real-life connection, compose thank-you notes as a class and individually whenever possible. Notes can be written for field trips, special events, or presentations performed at your school or to staff members who have worked in your classroom. Stock your writing center with materials to encourage the writing of thank-you notes among students. Include rubber stamps and stickers to add color and fun.

Display and Presentation

Students can share their cards and illustrations through an oral presentation to the class, in a small group, or with a partner. Place the cards on a bulletin board titled "Thanks for the Memories" to highlight these great adventure books.

Adventure Thank-You Note

Dear ______________________________________ and family,

Whether you sail the seven seas, visit a castle, or travel the Wild West, an adventure chapter book can make you feel a part of the action! In this book project, you will be thanking your book's characters for taking you along on their adventure.

Getting started:

You need the pattern page, markers or crayons, a 9" x 12" piece of colored construction paper for the outside of the card, and plain white paper for your written message. You may want a ruler and a pencil to make light lines to write on, along with an eraser to remove the lines after you are done writing.

Making your project:

1. Find a fiction chapter book with characters who go on an exciting adventure. Return the signed form at the bottom of the *How did I do?* page.

2. As you read, pay close attention to details of the setting and events that happen. Pick an event and pretend you were invited along by the characters.
3. Using your writing paper, draft a note to thank the characters of your story for including you in the event. Be sure to tell what happened and why you enjoyed it! Have an adult help you edit your thank-you note before writing your final copy on the pattern page.

4. Fold your construction paper in half and decorate it. Write "Thank You!" on the cover. Glue your note inside the card.
5. Use the photograph box on the pattern page to draw the setting and include important details of the event. Cut it out and glue it on the inside of the card's cover.
6. Bring your completed thank-you card to school.

Sharing your adventure thank-you note:

You will share your card with our class and tell us about the event you chose. We will display our cards so our class and visitors can enjoy them.

Adventure Thank-You Note

Pattern Page

Thank-You Note

Date ____________________

Dear ____________________,

____

____

____

____

____

Thank you so much!

Sincerely,

____
Your name

Photograph Box

Adventure Thank-You Note

How did I do?

My thank-you note describes an important event from the story.			
I wrote in complete sentences in my thank-you note.			
My card is neat and colorful.			
I gave the project my best effort.			
I brought my project to school on time.			

Did you read the book to your child or did your child read the book to you?

____

Other comments:

____

____

____

Comments from Teacher:

____

____

____

____

____

____

Please sign and return

The ____________________ family has received the information for the *Adventure Thank-You Note* project. We are aware that the project is due on ________________.

____

Parent Signature

Book Projects Word Bank

Chapter book—a book with many events, separated into parts called chapters.

Character traits—details about a character's physical appearance and personality.

Event—an important thing that happens in a story.

Setting—the main place where a story occurs.

Main character—the person or animal that is most involved in a story's events.

Plot—the order of events that take place in a story.

Problem—an issue that a character must solve to reach the end of a story.

Expository text—a nonfiction book filled with facts and information.

Sequence—the order of events that happen in a story—the beginning, middle, and end.

Solution—the way a character solves the main problem in a story.

Suggested Titles for Second Grade Readers

A Chair for My Mother by Vera B. Williams
A Tree Is a Plant by Clyde Robert Bulla
Abigail Takes the Wheel by Avi
Abiyoyo by Pete Seeger
Adventures of Taxi Dog by Debra Barracca
Amelia Bedelia by Peggy Parish
Arthur's Mystery Envelope by Marc Brown
Ben Franklin and His First Kite by Stephen Krensky
Breakout at the Bug Lab by Ruth Horowitz
Cloudy With a Chance of Meatballs by Judi Barrett
Henry and Mudge: The First Book by Cynthia Rylant
Junie B., First Graders: Boss of Lunch by Barbara Park
Keep the Lights Burning, Abbie by Connie Roop
Magic Tree House series by Mary Pope Osborne
Mr. Putter and Tabby Pick the Pears by Cynthia Rylant
Mrs. Piggle-Wiggle by Betty MacDonald
Pinky and Rex by James Howe
Sylvester and the Magic Pebble by William Steig
Tacky the Penguin by Helen Lester
The Drinking Gourd by F. N. Monjo
The Mitten by Jan Brett
The Velveteen Rabbit by Margery Williams